For ordering information please contact:

Willeo Publishing
702 Foxborough Sq. W.
Brentwood, Tennessee, 37027.

(615) 370-6413 or (800) 282-9266.

1st Edition
ISBN 0-9633662-3-8

Grief the Healer

spiritual reflections on the healing power of grief.

Jim McGregor

Cover and inside photographs by **Janie Bullard**

Willeo Publishing,
Brentwood, Tennessee

Contents

Acknowledgments

I wish to express my deep appreciation to my wife and soul-mate, Phyllis. Without her there would not have been a book. Her careful assemblage of this random group of contemplations, which had languished in my computer for five years, lent them order and coherence.

Thanks to Leigh Pettus for her constant encouragement and support.

Thanks to Janie Bullard for her exquisite photographs once again. Her creative work in my first book, *I Love You Enough to Let You Go* has brought many compliments from our readers throughout the years.

To the Reader

This random collection of short and simple thoughts of mine are about deaths of all kinds and the healing power of the grief process. A death could be the loss of a loved one, a relationship that has run its course, or even a way of life that is no longer feasible. My thoughts come largely from my life experiences.

Grief the Healer is meant to be browsed. Chances are that you will find something here that will speak to you. Maybe the short selections in the first section will suit your present needs; or maybe you will want to explore the longer version in the second section.

You may notice some duplication of material between the two versions; this is intentional. Often, the light bulb comes on, not the first time we see something that speaks to us, but the second or third time. Maybe this will happen for you here.

My wish for you is that your loss is made easier by something you read in this little book.

Jim McGregor

When I embrace grief . . .
when I put my arms around grief . . .
when I give up my unhealthy desires . . .
when I accept the darkness of the moment . . .
I will move from darkness into the light.

Part I

Random Selections

Grief

Grief is natural.
Grief is healthy.
Grief is normal.
Grief is healing.
Grief is mysterious.

Mystery

There is a mystery to grief.
Grief is not really grief.
Grief is healing.
Grief is the mysterious process of
moving from trauma to . . . peace and harmony.

Embrace grief

When I embrace grief . . .
when I put my arms around grief . . .
I will give up my unhealthy desires
and accept the darkness of the moment.
Then I will move from darkness into light.

Small healings

In the spirit of the ancient ones . . .
maybe I could simplify my grief
by breaking it down into smaller pieces.
Maybe then I will be able to transform
a small grief into a small healing.
Maybe this will be the first of many.

Small grievings

Grief comes in all sizes.
I will choose the small size
and see if I need more.

Denial

When I accept denial as a normal part
of the grief process . . .
I will gently move along the path
to wholeness.

Darkness

Pain comes out of darkness.
Grief comes out of light.
Grief feels like the air . . . nothing.
Grief is like the Great Mother.
I am held in her arms until . . .
I am ready to move on.

Great Mother

Pain and grief are intertwined.
Pain is visible . . . obvious.
Grief comes from a deeper source.
Grief is the Great Mother of all pain.
Thank you Great Mother for moving me . . .
from pain through grief.

From fear to serenity

Pain and grief and healing need each other.
They move me from fear to serenity.

The Divine

I accept your ending.
I accept your pain.
I accept you as a spiritual being.
I accept the unlimitedness of the . . .
Divine presence.

The journey

Life is a journey.
The flow of life and all its mysteries
have led me to accept the journey
as unexplainable . . . and spiritual.

Trust

When I trust the way of spirit
I no longer consider this death a loss.

Spirit

My spiritual self beckons me.
Come to the Great Mother . . .
for more.

Soul

Spiritual forgiveness is of the soul.
It has nothing to do with actions.

Acceptance

Spiritual love is universal healing.
When I reach a new level of acceptance
I can love all my life . . .
even the unlovable.

Free at last

I feel a spiritual presence.
I am finally free to move on.

Universal rhythm

There is an orderly natural process
constantly evolving.
Part of this natural process is death . . .
Death of plants and animals and . . .
Sometimes friends.
How simple.

Peace

When I accept death as being
in the natural order of things
there is no fear.
When there is no fear there is
peace, serenity and joy.

Fear

Why am I so afraid of the word death?
Why am I so afraid of dying?
Why am I so afraid of your death?
Perhaps I don't understand the universal
process . . . birth, life, death, and rebirth.
When I join the natural flow
I will have no fear.

Death

My birth came from spirit.
My body came from my birth . . . and spirit.
My life follows my birth with all its
pain and joy.
The death of my body will follow my life.
I will just go back to whence I came.

Beginnings

I now understand that all things end.
New beginnings arrive.
This is the way of the universal order.

Sometime

My body will surly die . . . sometime.
All things will surely die . . . sometime.
New things will take their place.
Spirit will never die.

Universal love

Death of love in the universal sense is
the death of all that is worthwhile.
There is no more.

Unimportant deaths

There are no unimportant deaths.
Each ending could lead to
a rebirth of infinite value.

The self

Death of the self often leads to
renewal and bliss.

The soul

Death of the soul is an illusion
and is never permanent.
Even so . . .
it is the ultimate loss.

Listening

You always had time to listen . . .
to the wind, the rain
and the sounds of the forest.
Now there are sounds of death.
You are listening.
You are at peace.
You are loved.

A treasure

One of my most treasured memories is of a
friend allowing me to share her death
experience as well as her lovely
spiritual presence. This memory is a part of
my being and I treasure it.

Memories

When you are truly gone . . .
it is in the natural order
to recall happy memories and
forgive the trials . . .
and finally reach our perfect relationship.
I let you go with absolute love.

Son

When I accept the reality of his death
I will honor my son by letting him go.
I will nurture my son
with a mother's gentle love.

Dishonor
My continuing grief could lead to my destruction.
I will not tarnish your memory with my destruction.
I will not dishonor you . . .
This is not the way of the Divine presence,
nor do I believe that it is your wish for me.

Honoring
Can I let his death be his alone?
Do I honor him by "dying" with him.

Pain
I am amazed at the peace and serenity
that I feel as I face my mother's death.
We have come through our pain before.
We will come through it again.
I am sad. I am lonesome. I am at peace.

My mother and I

My mother and I have shared a number of
endings, some pleasant, some not.
My mother and I . . .
no more strife . . . no more endings.

At last

At last . . . your perfect place.
At last . . . our perfect relationship.
At last . . . no conflict.

Closeness

The end is coming.
It will be soon.
Let's say goodbye.
No barriers . . .
a closeness beyond closeness.

Goodbye

My love for you is deep.
My love for you is free.
My love for you is everlasting.
Goodbye my love.

The "rock"

I have been the solid "rock."
My daughter is dead.
The rock has crumbled.

Emotions

There was a time when I thought it unmanly
to become emotional over losses.
Maybe I have changed.
Now I can cry.
Now I can let you see me cry.

Difficult
Your transition has been difficult . . .
and loving . . . and rewarding.

Family
How could my father's death have been a
beautiful family experience?
Easily.
We accepted death as one of
life's natural processes.
No resistance.

Forgiveness
The errors of the past are irreversible.
So I send you this message . . .
"Now that I have forgiven myself . . .
I forgive you."

Permission
I accept your forgiveness
with or without your permission.

Thank you

*I am grateful to you for allowing
me to share myself with you.
It is good for the soul.*

Sharing

*When I get glimpses of understanding
of you I feel great relief.
Thank you for sharing your self.*

Awareness

*Your rebirth . . .
your new awareness and your beautiful
presence are an important part of my life.
The joy I feel for you makes every day
more exciting.*

Misery

*This loss may be the end of your misery.
Your rebirth may be your new beginning.*

True friends

I have a loving support group . . .
True friends.
They are gifts from the spirit.
I am at peace.

Loving me

Loving myself will allow me to . . .
love my pain.
Pain cannot long survive when loved.

Beyond

There must be a place beyond
where peace and solitude and love prevail.
I am not sure when I will get there
but I have a deep knowing that I will.

Demanding

My demands have yielded no relief.
Maybe by demanding nothing
by becoming quiet and open
by listening to my inner voice
I will not need answers.
Maybe then I will know healing
and peace and love.

How strange

My experiences have sometimes been
traumatic.
My traumatic experiences have often been
blessings.
How strange.

Aloneness

I need some times of aloneness.

Self pity
I will remember the ugliness of self pity.
Then I will remember the beauty
of spiritual acceptance.

Untold joy
I now let you go in the spiritual sense . . .
knowing that this ending may lead to a
beautiful rebirth of untold joy.

Eternity
Eternity is now and forever.
Eternity is now forever.
I am in the now moment . . . forever.

Rebirth
There are no endings.
There is always a rebirth of some kind.

Misunderstandings

It is never too late to resolve
past misunderstandings.
There is a spiritual essence
to forgiveness . . . and understanding.

Closure

One of the wonderful gifts of spirit
is closure.
Closure creates space for a new beginning.
The ending of "this" so "that" can begin.

Self worth

Self pity can be mistaken for grief.
Self pity has to do with low self worth.
Self pity has no redeeming qualities.
Self pity provides no closure . . .
And no rebirth.

Feelings

It seems that we really don't know the depth of our feelings for someone until they are gone.

Limitation

Why would someone want me to live a limited life after they are gone?

Birth and death

Birth and death are ever present . . . sometimes traumatic . . . often a blessing.

Gentle way

The gentle way is less stressful.
The gentle way is easy.
The gentle way works.

Now
The place and time are here and now.
The past is over . . . and gone.

Gentle and hard
Some of us want everything to be quiet
and peaceful, but there is a hard side to
things as well.
The serene and gentle are not the only
occupants of the universal order.

Choices
Resist and lose.
Let go and win.
These are my choices.

Loving me
Loving myself allows me to love you.

Humility
In the universal sense
I am important . . .
But not omnipotent.

Soft and simple
Soft and gentle breezes . . .
nourish and protect all they touch.
Soft and simple lives . . .
nourish and protect all they touch.

Old age
I am feeling different now.
Old age feels more like a soft breeze
than a gale.
I am beginning to feel like the soft breeze
that blows and nourishes forever.

Finishing life

Finishing life with a flourish
is demanding.
Finishing life like a meandering stream
leaves plenty of space and . . .
invites others to share the experience.

Harmony

I am now free to float down the stream
of life in peace and harmony.

May your grievings be gentle and kind.

Part II

Mind

Yielding

Grief comes in all sizes.
I will choose the small size . . .
and see if I need more.

All grief is healing . . . if I am

open to its magical curative powers.

In the spirit of the ancient ones, maybe I could

simplify my grief by breaking it down into

smaller pieces. Then, I could begin to look at

my concerns one at a time.

Maybe this will be the first of many healings.

Trust

Grief is a time of healing . . .
when I trust the way things work.

I cannot expect to go through life free of
grief . . . the flow of the universe, although constant, is
nevertheless unpredictable. There would be no life without
death. They are both part of the universal process.

I will be at one with changes and I will accept the resulting
grief as healthy and in the natural order of things.

Then I will trust.

Feelings

Feelings can be trusted . . .
when I am at peace.

How does it feel . . .

when others no longer see you as perfect?

*How does it feel . . . when you realize that
your dreams were only fantasies?*

*How does it feel . . . when your dreams have come true and
they don't provide meaning and fulfillment?*

How does it feel?

*I will move into the spiritual realm and allow the past to
die a gentle death. I will accept the present moment and be
open and receptive to the birth of my new life.*

How does it feel . . . now?

At Last

I will no longer live like this.
I am no longer afraid.

Why am I so afraid?

There are some who are not afraid . . .
maybe they have looked inside, didn't like what
they saw, made the decision . . .
"I will no longer live like this."

I will join the "unafraid"
when I find the Way . . . my way.

Then . . . I will not be afraid.

Denying Grief

I was strong . . . so I thought.
I did not feel anything . . . so I thought.

Why grieve . . .

When my mother died, was I not supposed to feel anything? I didn't . . . or so I thought.

When my friends all around me were being killed or lost in war, was I not supposed to feel anything? I didn't . . . or so I thought.

When my marriage dissolved, was I not supposed to feel anything? This time I did . . . and I fell apart.

I also recovered.

I now accept that denial is a natural response to any trauma.

I now understand the consequences of denial and will not resist. I will accept denial as a normal part of the grief process and gently move beyond it.

Contemplate Grief

Worrying and demanding answers
are the way of the neurotic.

Letting go and accepting
are the way of the contemplative.

I have a choice . . . neurotic . . . contemplative

. . . or somewhere in between.

I am consumed by my grief.

I believe I will change from an intellectual who must have all the answers, to a contemplative who knows there are no rational answers, and therefore, demands nothing.

By demanding nothing . . .
by becoming quiet and open . . . by listening to my inner voice . . . maybe I will not need answers.

Maybe then I will know healing, peace, and love.

Sharing Grief

When I get glimpses of understanding . . . I feel great relief.

Thank you for sharing.

It is easy to be self-centered and depressed

when I am in periods of darkness.

Grieving is healthy as long as the grief is

compassionate and useful.

I will be gentle and forgive myself . . .

remembering that you are

grieving with me at this time.

Unmanly

There was a time when
I thought it unmanly to become
emotional over losses or endings.

I can now cry . . .
I can now let you see me cry.

I had been strong, or so I thought . . .
at least I showed no emotion at stressful times.

Things are different now . . . the turbulence
of my life brought me down.

I am grateful for all my years . . .
especially for the beauty of the present moment.

I am grateful to you for allowing me to share myself
with you. It is good for the soul.

Heroic

*Heroic actions sometimes dull
the fear of unworthiness.*

*Heroic actions are sometimes
tragic for the hero.*

I have no problem with the idea of death . . .
I have faced death many times. I do have a problem facing
the fact of my impending death.

The very accomplishments that filled me with pride
now seem empty and meaningless.

There must be a place beyond all this where peace
and solitude and love prevail.

I am not sure how to get there, but I have a deep
knowing that Oneness is already on the way.

Self-Pity

*I remember the feeling of
self pity*

*I will remember the beauty of
spiritual grief.*

Grief is spiritual and has to do with the soul.

*True grief is born out of loss . . . has a healthy life . . .
experiences a natural ending . . . and a rebirth.*

*Self-pity is sometimes mistaken for grief.
There is often no beginning event . . . no life of its own . . .
no closure . . . and no rebirth.*

*Self-pity has to do with low self-esteem and has no
redeeming qualities.*

*Thinking of the beauty and life-giving of spiritual grief
makes me feel warm and secure.*

Pain Is Real

*Pain can drive one
to excessive behavior.*

*Pain can lead one to grief,
to healing, and to renewal.*

Pain is the great leveler . . .

There are those of us who react to pain with excesses . . .
addictions, broken relationships and geographical cures.

There are those of us who never give up our excesses.

There are those of us who give up the excesses . . .
accept the healing pain . . . move through the beauty of
healthy grief . . . and no longer ask for answers.

Friend

I invite you to share your anger with me.

I am your friend.

All forms of death may seem unfair —
certainly they are painful.

I was once angry at God and felt guilty;
I now recognize that I was angry at myself.

I am here for you should you choose to
share your feelings and frustrations with me.

Fear

Fear of the unknown
is natural and protective.

The greatest fear is that of the unknown.

When I am centered and at one with the Divine power, fear of the unknown is no longer fear as I have perceived it. It is an opportunity to move to a higher level of being.

I am now willing to trust my instincts, knowing that the fear of death is natural and is a necessary part of growth.

Why Am I So Afraid

I will be ready . . . some day
to let go of my fear.

Why am I so afraid of the word death?
Why am I so afraid of dying?

I must not yet have let go of my obsession to hang on . . .
to possess . . . to control.

I must not yet have joined the natural flow of the universe.

Am I ready . . . maybe . . . but not now.

However, I am beginning to feel a slight breeze —
a fresh new breath of hope.

How Wonderful

I am now watchful . . .

*Fear and anger are
no longer significant.*

How wonderful . . .

Fear, and anger were my constant companions . . .

Shear terror and rage arrived with any tragedy . . .
perceived or real.

Then came my metamorphosis . . .

I listened and found the "whatever it is" that let me
see trauma and tragedy as a part of the
human experience, not as an aberration.

I am now watchful . . .
I yield to the pain and fear . . .

Fear and anger are still present . . .
at a manageable level . . . Fear and anger are
no longer significant.

How wonderful

Body

Death Of The Body

*Birth, life, and death
is a universal process . . .*

*Birth, life, and death are each
beginnings . . . not endings.*

Your physical death or the thought of it

has been too painful and frightening to accept.

This is the human side of me at work.

I now let go of my insecurities, fears, and demands for an

unnatural solution to the natural problem of your death.

The spiritual side of me has already let you go.

This is in the natural order of things.

This is the way of the heart . . . not of the mind.

Reality not illusion.

The Randomness Of Death

Death is random . . .

I did not understand.

Why does lightening strike certain trees . . . young or old?

Why do tornados wipe out certain towns
and leave others unscathed?

Why do famines strike some countries
while others enjoy abundance?

Why me . . . what happened to me?

I now understand that there is a randomness
to the natural order of the universe that is consistent,
definite, and always present.

I am now free to float on the stream of life
and death in peace and harmony.

Time

*It seems that we really don't know
the depth of our feelings for someone
until there is an ending.*

There is time for goodbyes . . .

they are really not goodbyes . . . just changes.

There is time for reflection . . .

There is time for myself . . .

There is time . . . eons condensed into the now moment.

There is time.

Destruction

My continued grief could lead
to my destruction . . .

I will not dishonor you by my
destruction.

Each time that there has been a "tragic ending" in my life
I have felt extreme pain. Then, as I learned about
acceptance and forgiveness . . . and time passed,
I inevitably found a new life.

Let me remember that the healing power of the
Divine is ever present. When I become ready to accept the
gifts of the spirit, I will once again find the strength and
serenity that I have known in the past.

Mother
Another ending . . .

My mother and I have shared a number of endings . . . some pleasant . . . some not.

My mother and I . . . no more strife . . . no more endings.

My mother is dying.

I am amazed at the peace and serenity that I feel,
knowing that she will be in her perfect place.
And most of all knowing that our relationship
is not over . . . it will just be different.

My mother and I have come through our pain in the past
and we will come through again . . . each in our own way.

I am sad . . . I am lonesome . . . I am grateful.

My Son

I will honor my departed son by letting him go.

I will nurture my departed son
with a Mother's gentle love . . .

when I accept the reality of his death.

My son is dead . . .

This man-child of mine was my life . . .
in his death I have died.

Do I honor him by dying with him?

I experienced the pain of my son's birth . . .
I gave him a Mother's gentle love . . . I will afford my son
the same gentle love . . . when I am ready.

My Daughter

I have been the solid "rock" . . .

My daughter is dead . . .

The rock has crumbled.

My daughter is dead . . .

My insides feel like stone . . . I want to run away.

I am the rock . . .

I am not the rock.

I want to cry on someone's shoulder.

Maybe I will try sharing a small part of my grief.
Could it be that you are waiting for me?

Just a few tears.

Soulmate

My love for you is deep.

My love for you is free.

My love for you will continue.

Goodbye My Love . . .

You have moved into the world of the spirit.

I will miss you . . . I am sad . . .

I am at peace.

Letting Go

When I accept death as in the natural order
there is no fear.

When there is no fear
there is peace . . . serenity . . . and joy.

There was once a caring medical and spiritual healer
who was sought out by many who were terminally ill.
His greatest challenge came when his dying father
refused the necessary treatments.
"All I could do was help him die a joyful death."

There are those of us who accept death as a
basic part of the natural order. Having processed the grief
and loneliness, one can see the positive side of it.

I invite you to accept that which is right there
in front of you . . . and let go.

Perfect

At last . . . your perfect place.

At last . . . our perfect relationship.

At last . . . no conflict.

Your death is real and I cannot change that.

In the past our relationship has survived the usual difficulties. It was stressful at times.

Regardless of our earthly circumstances, there will always be our perfect relationship . . . enmeshed with the spiritual and universal love that makes all things whole.

I miss you . . . I wish that you were here by my side but I am grateful for the opportunity of sharing this new phase of our oneness.

Thank you for our past. Thank you for our new and perfect relationship.

Spirit

Beginnings

I now understand that all things end . . . new beginnings arrive. This is the way of the universal order.

It is in the natural order of the universe
for all things to move on.

I have experienced the deaths of loved ones . . . as well as
the deaths of old beliefs, emotions, and relationships. I now
know that these endings were in the natural order.

All things end . . . new beginnings arrive.

This is the way of the divine.

Spiritual Journey

Life is a journey . . .

unexplainable . . . spiritual.

Life is a journey . . . and death in any form
is a part of life's journey. The flow of life and all its
mysteries have led me to accept the journey as
unexplainable . . . and spiritual.

Mystery

Grief is mysterious.

Grief is healing.

There is a mystery to grief.

Grief is not really grief . . . grief is healing.

Grief is that mysterious process of moving from trauma of all kinds to peace, love and joy.

True healing is hidden in darkness waiting for me to accept the present moment.

God

I don't know why
God doesn't take the pain away.

When I am grieving . . .

Why doesn't God take the pain away?

Some of us have stopped asking for answers.

*The randomness of death
make the questions unanswerable.*

I don't know why God doesn't take the pain away.

Aloneness
*I need some times
of aloneness.*

There are times when I need to be alone.
The spiritual part of me calls me into deep silence.

Then, there comes a time when I must let go of my grief
and move on to the joys of living.

Aloneness does not always mean being alone.

Spiritual aloneness means
being one with the Divine . . . never alone again.

Stream Of Life

Finishing life with a flourish is demanding.

Finishing life like a meandering stream
leaves plenty of space and invites others
to share the experience.

I am considered strange.

I always have time to listen to the wind,
the thunder and the sounds of the forest.

I have been in the stream of life the easy way . . .
no resistance. Flowing with the stream from its source . . .
my birth, to the sea . . . my impending death,

I am at peace . . . I am loved.

Guilt

Guilt and spiritual forgiveness
cannot coexist . . .

It is never too late to resolve past misunderstandings
since there is a spiritual flavor to forgiveness.

Spiritual forgiveness has to do with souls . . .
it has nothing to do with actions.

I will remember that a beautiful, spiritual me is the most
important gift I can make to the universe.

Now that I have forgiven myself, I forgive you.

I accept your forgiveness, with or without your permission.

Answers

I looked for my answers
in all the wrong places . . .

answers are already here.

Listen . . .

Deep listening is where my answers are.
I now let go in the spiritual sense knowing that my loss,
in whatever form, may be a beautiful rebirth
of untold joy . . . should I choose it.

Could I love me, support me, honor me more?

Painful Past

I will love you . . .

until you can love your painful past . . .

enough to let it go.

Love is a beautiful healer and, in the spiritual sense,
it may be the only true healing force.

So it seems that my part in this experience
of yours is to love you . . . and to apply the healing magic
of love to the death of your painful past.

Acceptance

I accept you.

I accept your endings . . .

I accept your pain . . .

I accept you as a spiritual being . . .

I accept your limitations . . .

I accept the unlimitedness of the Divine presence . . .

Spirit
How perfect . . .

My birth came from spirit.

My body came from my birth . . . and . . . spirit.

My life follows my birth . . . with all its pain and joy.

The death of my body will follow my life.

My rebirth will send me back to spirit . . .

I will just go back to where I came from . . .

How perfect . . .

Loving Grief

Spiritual love is the universal healing force.

I can love all things in my life . . .
even the unlovable.

The serene one said

that when grief consumes my life,

I just need to love it more.

I will love my grief more and

more until it becomes . . . natural and healthy . . .

and healing.

Peace be still . . .

The Way
There is no ending . . .

All things will surely die . . . sometime . . .
· new things will take their place.

Spirit will never die . . . nothing will take its place.

There is death but no final ending . . . this is
The Way of the universal order.

The Light

Pain and grief and healing need each other . . .

to move me from darkness to light.

Pain feels real and solid . . .

Pain comes out of darkness . . .

Grief feels like the air . . .

Grief comes out of light . . .

Healing comes from Nowhere . . .

Healing is the Great Mother of renewal.

Comfort

Thank you Great Mother for moving me
from pain through grief.

I am healing . . .

Pain and grief are intertwined . . .

Pain is visible . . . obvious.
Grief comes from another source.
Grief is the Great Mother of pain.

Grief, in the secular sense
provides a way of moving from pain to painless.

Grief, in the spiritual sense, is a veiled source of comfort.

Spiritual grief is ever present and
is our constant source of compassion . . . not pain.

Gentle

Temporary relief is better than none.

My spiritual self beckons me . . .

come to the Great Mother . . .

for more.

I tried everything that seemed useful . . . silence,
detachment, letting go, meditation . . . and prayer.

The results were temporary and partial
until I accepted a gentle ending for my grief.

By moving further along the spiritual path,
those few grievings that come into my life today
are softer and more gentle.

Softer

My experiences have sometimes been traumatic.

My traumatic experiences have often been blessings.

How strange . . .

Birth is a trauma and a blessing . . .

Death is a trauma and a blessing . . .

Birth and death are ever present . . . often traumatic
. . . often a blessing.

To lean toward the softer side . . . the side of the Great
Mother . . . is the way.

Desireless

My strong desire for peace . . .
love . . . and . . . serenity delayed my gift of . . .

peace, love, and serenity.

I have appeared peaceful

even when there was no peace inside.

As time passed, a feeling of peace arrived

. . . a gift from spirit.

Had I become desireless years ago,

maybe I would not have had to wait for the incredible gifts

of spirit . . . peace . . . love . . . serenity.

Waiting

The gentle way is easy

and less stressful.

The gentle way works

I was not healing . . . so I decided to wait.

Being open to the healing gift of spirit . . . has moved me along the path of beauty and serenity . . .

Waiting works . . . it still doesn't make sense.

Closure

One of the beautiful gifts of spirit is closure . . .

the ending of "this" so "that" can begin.

Closure creates space for the new beginning.

*Those things that seemed perfect were perfect for the
moment . . . there has always been more.*

Why would someone live a limited life after an ending?

*When you are truly gone . . . it is in the natural order to
bask in the happy memories, forgive the trials, and finally
reach a perfect relationship.*

If it is over it is over.

I let you go with unconditional love.

Part III

Beyond Grief

Grief from the heart . . . freeing.

Society establishes boundaries

for proper expressions of grief.

There is another way . . . the way beyond all others.

Compassionate grief comes from within.

The way beyond is very comfortable for those who are in

accord with the natural order of things.

This is the way of the heart.

Death's Significance

There are no unimportant deaths . . .
each ending could lead to a rebirth
of inestimable value.

I think of those who have recovered from complete emotional breakdown and have risen to new heights of consciousness. They have brought untold good to the world.

I think of the breakdown of relationships between nations and the effect that this has had on the history of the planet.

These are deaths of major proportions. However, those deaths that each of us experience as individual parts of the Whole are also major events, and have unknown influences on the natural order of things.

There are no unimportant deaths . . . all deaths are a part of the spiritual realm. They should be viewed as such.

Taking Credit
Humility leads to serenity.

My need for recognition impedes my humility.

I am grieving over lost opportunities. How sick!

Do I not remember that success and failure are only opposites of each other . . . that the illusion of success I am grieving over might have been only a fantasy?

Maybe it is time for me to give up my need for recognition and forget about taking credit.

Hanging On

Some things I wanted . . .

Some things I needed . . .

There is a difference.

I have gone down the wrong path . . .

I have collected a big car, a big house, lavish surroundings, expensive habits . . . and a tremendous debt.

Things are different now . . . there is the pain of barely hanging on. I cannot give up my lifestyle.

Or can I? Maybe all will be taken away. Will I then have a peaceful heart or will I make the same mistake again?

The Pain Of Death

You won't be here any more . . .

That frightens me.

Whether it is death of your body or some other loss,
the "you" that I know will no longer be here.
That frightens me.

I will have to start over again.

I will look for strength from spirit and be open to the
healing grace that is there for all of us.

I am no longer frightened.

Here And Now

The place and time are here and now.

The past is over . . . and gone.

The place and the time are here and now.

*That which can be dealt with is right here
in front of us . . . now . . . nothing else matters.*

*Maybe now is the time that you have been waiting for.
Maybe now is the time to accept that which you
already know . . . the painful past is over.*

*There is no magic formula for letting go of the past. Each
of us must do this in our own time and in our own way.*

Homeless

We are all homeless at times . . . spiritually.

Some of us are homeless

. . . no house . . . no warmth . . . no food .

Some of us are homeless

. . . no house . . . no warmth . . . no food and . . .

No spirit . . .

My Job

It is time to go to work . . .

No place to go . . . nothing to do.

No job . . . no self worth.

How awful!

I lost my job . . . my self esteem . . . my ego.

I was not at fault; conditions, people, or circumstances
destroyed me . . . so I thought.

My rebirth has happened
. . . my fragile, arrogant ego has given way to a more
humble acceptance of myself . . . my shallow self esteem
has deepened into a knowing beyond all knowing.

I am at peace and I have a job that I love.
This is my experience.

Endings allow space for new beginnings . . .
rebirths that are healing, positive, and life-giving.

Money

Money was not the problem;

I was the problem.

Now . . .

No problem.

My money was my master
and I was my money's slave. Lack of money made me feel
desperate. I lost my money . . . and me.

I have grieved over my loss of money and my part in it
long enough. I have learned of humility and powerlessness.

I now rest in the spirit of the Universe
and am ready for the truly important days of my life,
however few they may be.

The Edge
Challenging the odds

I have stretched the limits.

Disaster was just a step away . . .
fear and pain were my constant companions.

Living on the edge was the way of those I admired.
Living on the edge became my way.

Living on the edge was thrilling, rewarding . . . and empty.

I am different now.

As I grieve the loss of my old self,
I listen for my place in the universal flow.

The healing power of grief is good for me.

Choices

Resist and lose . . .

let go and win . . .

These are my choices.

Pain is ruthless when resisted . . . it always wins.

Pain does not win when I cease to resist.

Am I a simple soul who resists giving up my pain?

Or am I a simple soul who finally lets go and moves beyond my pain . . . and win?

Abandonment

You left and I was abandoned.

I have experienced a rebirth.

Abandonment is no longer abandonment.

I will never be abandoned again.

Leaving no longer means abandonment.

I have found a sense of well being as a result of my
spiritual growth . . . I have let go of my dependence on you.

I am grateful for all the wonderful times we have had
together . . . tomorrow is beyond my control.

Aloneness is no longer abandonment.

To My Dad

My childhood is missing.

My Dad was missing
. . . not missing . . . just unavailable.

Where were you Dad when we needed you . . . when Mother
started her problems . . . how could you leave me to take
charge of what you could not control?

I am grieving my lost childhood and
will allow the grief to run its course. I will not let my life
be consumed by the grief.

The wise one says to gradually let go of the past,
live in the present, and move into the spiritual realm.
There is no hurry and no correct way.

I will be gentle with myself
. . . with Mother . . . and you, Dad.

I am grieving, but I am at peace.

Old Beliefs

Beliefs can grow old and stale . . .

New beliefs can be fresh and exciting.

Death of old beliefs is in the natural order of the universe.

It took a serious traumatic experience
for this beautiful change to arrive for me.

The acceptance of death of old beliefs as being
in the natural order, instead of an admission of failure,
will open the way for the exciting rebirth.

This rebirth can lead to peace and joy
. . . and my true self.

Relationships

Our relationship will inevitably change.

I have come to believe that relationships die

and are reborn, even with the same person.

When I think of the beginning excitement of a new

relationship, dying into the birth of a more profound one,

acceptance of each other's differences is simple and worthy.

All relationships will change.

This is the way of the natural order of things.

Soft Breezes
I now know the softer way . . .

Soft breezes nourish and protect all they touch.

Simple and "soft" lives nourish and protect all they touch.

I am beginning to feel like the soft breeze . . .
that will blow and nourish forever.

I am feeling different now . . .
spirit works in wondrous ways.

Life feels more like a soft breeze than a gale.

For Myself

I have experienced it again . . .

a different kind of closeness . . .

no barriers.

Closeness beyond closeness.

Significant changes, including death, are difficult . . . for the one who is changing and for those who love them.

One of my most beautiful memories is that of a friend allowing me the privilege of sharing her death experience as well as her lovely spiritual presence.
This memory is a part of my being and I treasure it.

So I will be ever present during your transition . . . for you . . . and for myself.

Peace And Harmony

Your flowering is a sight to behold.

Your rebirth, your new awareness, and your beautiful

presence are an important part of my life today.

You are a gift . . . you are an important part of my life.

I love you and I honor you.

I feel a spiritual presence.

I am free to move on.

About the Author

Jim McGregor was born in Medicine Hat, Alberta, Canada, a third generation of prominent Aberdeen Angus cattle breeders. He grew up in New York State and on the Eastern Shore of Maryland. After serving in WWll as a lead bomber pilot, Jim had a variety of careers, including food service manager, cattle breeder, and financial salesman before he turned to writing in his middle sixties.

Jim is the author of three published books: *I Love You Enough to Let You Go*, *I Love Me Enough to Let Me Go*, and *The Tao of Recovery*. His works come from personal experiences and quiet meditation.

After a difficult divorce and loss of a business, Jim retreated to the north Georgia mountains for a year of solitude. It was that life-changing experience, along with involvement in recovery groups and the discovery of the ancient philosophy, Tao Te Ching, that inspired him to write.

After living in Atlanta for thirty five years, Jim, along with his wife Phyllis, moved to Tennessee.

He treasures the peace and serenity he has found sharing the inspirational messages that come to him.